BASIC COURSEBUILDING

by

Maureen Summers

Illustrations by

Carole Vincer

KENILWORTH PRESS

First published in Great Britain by
The Kenilworth Press Limited,
Addington, Buckingham, MK18 2JR

© The Kenilworth Press Limited 1991
Reprinted 1992, 1994, 1996

British Library Cataloguing in Publication Data
A catalogue record for this book is available from the British Library.

ISBN 1-872082-06-8

Typeset by DP Photosetting, Aylesbury, Bucks

Printed in Great Britain by Westway Offset, Wembley

CONTENTS

Introduction

It is always more fun to return home from a show having jumped a clear round, rather than having been eliminated. So often the poor horse gets the blame when actually he may have been presented with unfair problems by an inexperienced course designer.

Building a safe and jumpable show-jumping course requires an awareness of many factors: for example, the size and stride lengths of the animals involved; the level of experience of the horses and riders; the terrain; the size of the jumping area; the safe utilisation of available materials.

The aim of this book is to provide a ready reference for anyone who builds a course, be it a few practice fences at home or a course at a show. It offers easy-to-follow guidelines to distances between combinations and other jumps, with helpful ideas for the safe layout and erection of show-jumping courses for ponies and horses of different sizes, abilities and experience.

Jumping at home

It is important to build your practice fences at home as well as possible, as this is the nursery school for the inexperienced horse or pony. Here he can learn that jumping is fun, that coloured fences will not harm him, and that combination obstacles are not a problem because he can jump through them happily without altering his stride.

Later, distances can be altered a fraction to teach him to lengthen and shorten his stride; then small courses can be built in preparation for his first show.

The fences themselves, and the distances between them, should bear as much resemblance as possible to those he will meet in the ring. A few brightly painted, solidly constructed fences will be of greater value than piles of logs and twigs.

The jumps should be easily approached, and if you don't possess a measuring tape, space out the fences so that there are multiples of *four* of your strides (taking care that your own strides measure roughly 3ft/90cm long) between any jumps that are placed in a line close together. This will ensure that there are no tricky distances.

It is essential that only safe materials are used. If you want to make use of any old 40-gallon oil drums – which are handy both as fillers and as alternative wing stands – make sure that they are reasonably sound and free from rust. Straw bales must be tightly packed, so that there is no danger of the horse's leg being caught in the baler twine.

The frame of a jump

A course of show jumps is made up of approximately eight to ten individual obstacles, each one made up of a **frame**, which determines the shape and dimensions required, and the **infill**, which makes the obstacle more appealing to the eye of the spectator and assists the horse in varying degrees, depending on the arrangement of the material.

Cups should fit snugly round the upright. They are made of either metal or plastic.

Pillars can be built with holes to support jump cups, or without, simply to stand at the ends of walls.

Poles are generally 12ft (3.65m) long and are often painted in bright colours. Mixing different coloured poles in the same jump can be unsightly.

Bolts: for safety, care must be taken to ensure that the sharp edges on the nuts are on the back of the wing, away from the approaching horse.

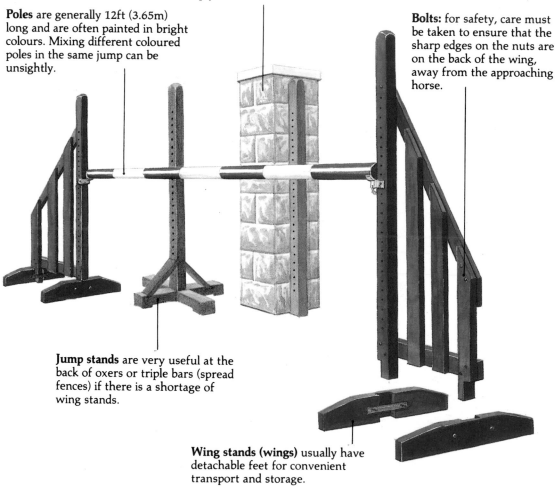

Jump stands are very useful at the back of oxers or triple bars (spread fences) if there is a shortage of wing stands.

Wing stands (wings) usually have detachable feet for convenient transport and storage.

The shape of the frame

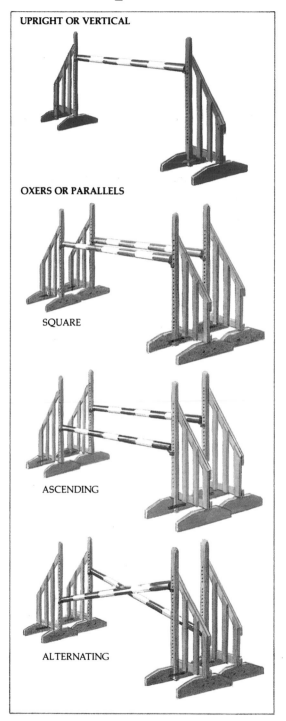

UPRIGHT OR VERTICAL

OXERS OR PARALLELS

SQUARE

ASCENDING

ALTERNATING

There are three basic shapes of jump:
Upright or vertical – consisting of one pair of wings, with poles and fillers in the same vertical plane.

Oxer or parallel – these consist of two pairs of wings. They may be: (a) 'ascending', with the front pole lower than the back pole, which is easiest to jump; (b) 'square', with the front and back poles level (but maker sure that the back pole is visible to the horse as he must know what he is being asked to jump); (c) 'alternating', with 'crossed' poles.

Staircases are usually triple bars, consisting of three pairs of wings, with the poles getting progressively higher. A convex appearance is easier to jump than one that is flat; a concave construction should never be used. Staircases can also be built with a small filler replacing the front pole.

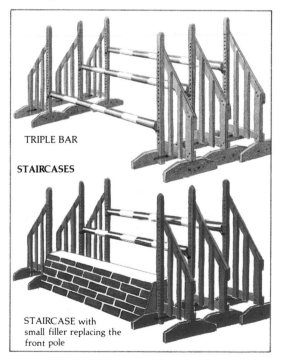

TRIPLE BAR

STAIRCASES

STAIRCASE with small filler replacing the front pole

Filling-in material

PLANK

PANEL

LADDER

HURDLE

BALES

BARRELS

BRUSH

SMALL WALL

ARCH WALL OR VIADUCT

BROKEN WALL

PICKET FENCE

WATER BRUSH

There is a vast selection of potential filling-in material, and plenty of room for improvisation too. How this material is used will determine the difficulty of the jump. If solidly filled, the fence will encourage bold, confident jumping; whereas a more open, or gappy, jump will not impress the horse as much and will need the skill of the rider to persuade the horse to negotiate it carefully.

The horse will judge his take-off from the **groundline**, which should never, therefore, be set back from the foremost vertical plane. A filler set in front of the jump will assist the horse to make a more rounded, easier jump, whilst gates, hanging panels, planks etc. require a greater degree of accuracy.

Never set a groundline back from the front poles, as this creates a false groundline, making a trap for the horse.

Complete, individual fences, such as large walls and different types of gate, make for variety in the course, both for the horse and the spectator.

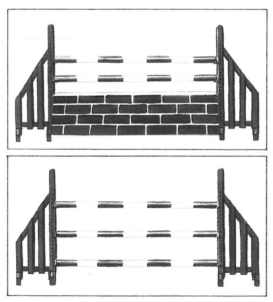

The horse will look, see and respect the solid fence at the top, but would pay less attention to the gappy one below it.

Safety

Using the advice and materials already shown it is possible to build a full course. Every precaution must be taken to ensure that the horse is not hurt in any way. If there is a shortage of fillers and improvisation is necessary, take extra care when using non-purpose-built equipment.

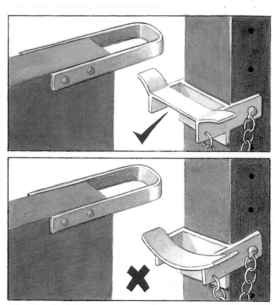

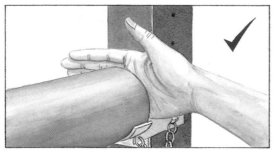

Make sure that there is room for your hand between the end of the pole and the upright, so that the pole will fall easily and cannot jam.

Planks, ladders, gates and panels must be placed on flat cups. Cups which are not in use must be removed from the wings as they are a danger.

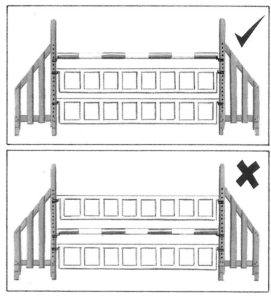

Barrels and poles on the ground should be wedged or pegged. On windy days gates will swing, so a ground peg should be used to prevent this.

Ladders and panels must always have a pole above them as they are far too heavy a piece of equipment for the horse to hit.

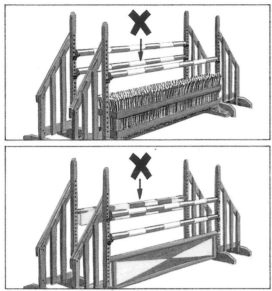

Never put anything other than a single pole on the back of an oxer or triple bar. Never stand or hang any form of filler under it.

Never put pillars at the back of a spread fence. Pillars do not fall as easily as wings and could bring down a horse who misjudged the jump.

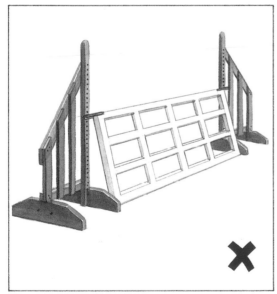

Never lean a gate to reduce its height as it will become wedged. Replace it with poles until the classes require the higher fence.

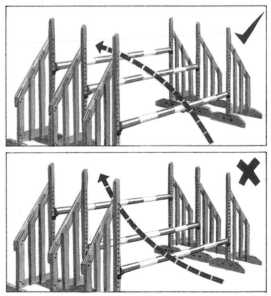

Triple bars should *never* be built with a concave appearance. A flat triple bar is difficult to jump; a convex slope will help the horse.

Double and treble combinations

Double and treble combinations consist of two or three jumps in a line with not more than two non-jumping strides between each element. They offer a test of the horse's training, and at the beginning of his career there should be 'true' distances (average natural stride lengths) between them and no nasty surprises.

The table below is a guide to the basic distances between fences set out with one and two non-jumping strides. Many factors affect the horse's or pony's stride, and the conditions on the day have to be taken into consideration.

A horse's stride will **shorten** by up to 1ft (30cm) if: (a) it is muddy; (b) the jumping area is confined; (c) he is going uphill; (d) he is going away from home. Where these conditions prevail use the shorter distances given in the table below.

A horse's stride will **lengthen** by up to 1ft (30cm) if: (a) the going is springy; (b) any downhill slopes are gentle (steep slopes tend to make a horse 'prop'); (c) he is going towards home; (d) the jumping area is large and open. Where these conditions prevail use the longer distances given in the table below.

For jumps less than 3ft (90cm) high, shorten the distances slightly so that the horse is not encouraged to jump long and flat.

	ONE NON-JUMPING STRIDE		
Over 14.2hh	7.30m–7.90m (24'–26')	7.15m–7.60m (23' 6"–25')	7m–7.60m (23'–25')
14.2hh	6.55m–7.45m (21' 6"–24' 6")	6.55m–7.15m (21' 6"–23' 6")	6.55m–7.15m (21' 6"–23' 6")
13.2hh	6.25m–7m (20' 6"–23')	NOT USED	NOT USED
Over 14.2hh	7.45m–7.75m (24' 6"–25' 6")	7m–7.30m (23'–24')	6.85m–7.30m (22' 6"–24')
14.2hh	6.55m–7.45m (21' 6"–24' 6")	NOT USED	NOT USED
13.2hh	6.25m–7m (20' 6"–23')	NOT USED	NOT USED
Over 14.2hh	7.45m–7.90m (24' 6"–26')	7m–7.45m (23'–24' 6")	6.85m–7.45m (22' 6"–24' 6")
14.2hh	6.55m–7.45m (21' 6"–24' 6")	NOT USED	NOT USED
13.2hh	6.25m–7m (20' 6"–23')	NOT USED	NOT USED

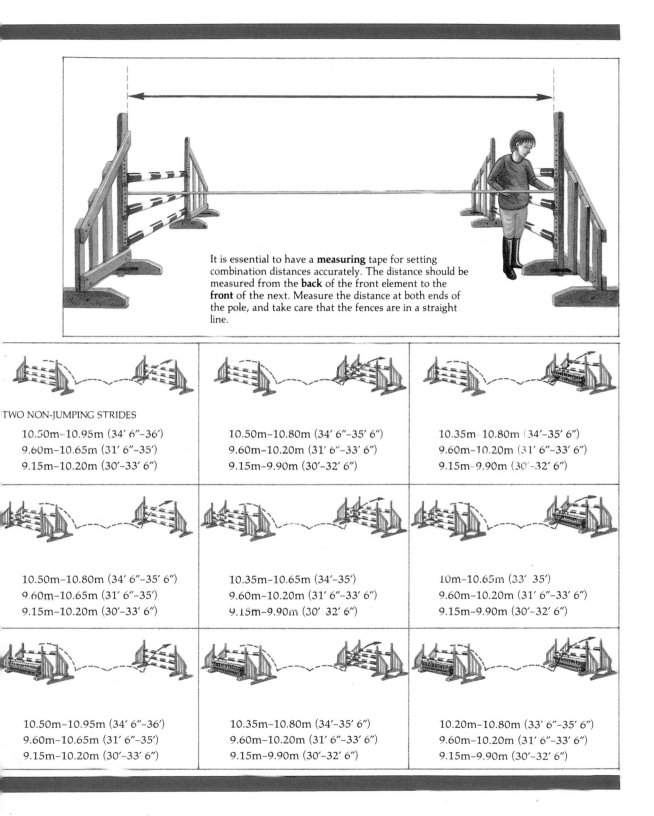

It is essential to have a **measuring** tape for setting combination distances accurately. The distance should be measured from the **back** of the front element to the **front** of the next. Measure the distance at both ends of the pole, and take care that the fences are in a straight line.

TWO NON-JUMPING STRIDES

10.50m–10.95m (34' 6"–36')
9.60m–10.65m (31' 6"–35')
9.15m–10.20m (30'–33' 6")

10.50m–10.80m (34' 6"–35' 6")
9.60m–10.20m (31' 6"–33' 6")
9.15m–9.90m (30'–32' 6")

10.35m–10.80m (34'–35' 6")
9.60m–10.20m (31' 6"–33' 6")
9.15m–9.90m (30'–32' 6")

10.50m–10.80m (34' 6"–35' 6")
9.60m–10.65m (31' 6"–35')
9.15m–10.20m (30'–33' 6")

10.35m–10.65m (34'–35')
9.60m–10.20m (31' 6"–33' 6")
9.15m–9.90m (30'–32' 6")

10m–10.65m (33'–35')
9.60m–10.20m (31' 6"–33' 6")
9.15m–9.90m (30'–32' 6")

10.50m–10.95m (34' 6"–36')
9.60m–10.65m (31' 6"–35')
9.15m–10.20m (30'–33' 6")

10.35m–10.80m (34'–35' 6")
9.60m–10.20m (31' 6"–33' 6")
9.15m–9.90m (30'–32' 6")

10.20m–10.80m (33' 6"–35' 6")
9.60m–10.20m (31' 6"–33' 6")
9.15m–9.90m (30'–32' 6")

Do's and don'ts for combinations

Sometimes horses and ponies are entered in the same class. If they are, the distance inside the combination must be built for the horse as he would be unable to fit his stride into a much smaller space. This will mean that the distance will probably be too great for the smaller-striding pony, so to ensure his safety the second element must be an upright, not a spread. If he is forced to put in two short strides instead of one normal stride, it will cause his jump to be more up and down instead of up and along, which could cause him to land on the back pole of a spread.

Always put the most imposing filler at the front of a combination. If it is placed later on, it may take the horse's eye away from the part on which he should be concentrating.

At this level it is inadvisable to build triple bars in combinations.

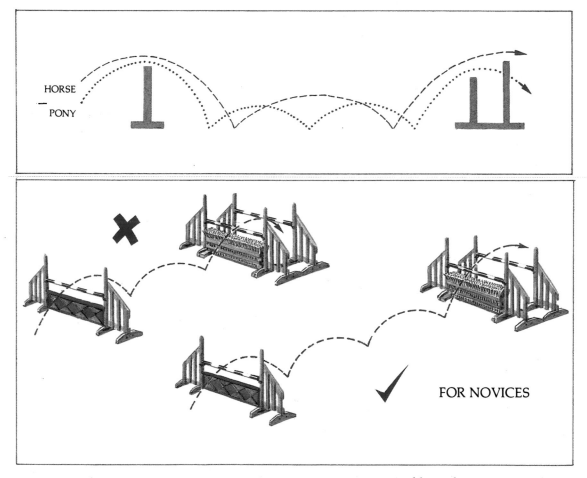

HORSE
PONY

FOR NOVICES

For novice classes it is wiser to use an upright, rather than an oxer, as the second fence in a combination, then if a mistake is made jumping in, the upright coming out will not present a problem. If an oxer is used, it should come after two non-jumping strides. This gives the horse more time to recover from a mistake.

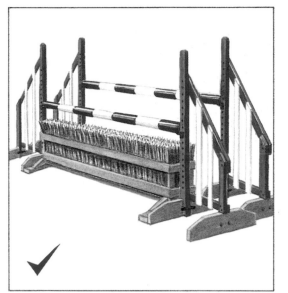

The easiest jump into a combination is an attractive, ascending spread. Anything too startling, or a very upright fence, will 'back the horse off'. This will cause him to land more steeply than he should, which will make him reach for the next stride or put in an extra one.

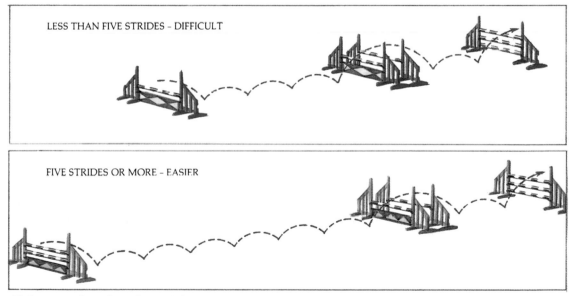

If there are less than five strides in a line before a combination, this can present a problem. If a horse makes a mistake at the beginning of the line, he will be in trouble for the rest of it, as there is not enough room for recovery.

Planning the course

It is important to spend an hour or so at the 'drawing board' pre-planning the courses for the show. The schedule will show how many classes there are, and if they have jumps-off (BSJA Table A.3).

It would be very boring for all concerned if everyone had to jump the same track, so try to work out a plan which, with only a little moving of jumps and maybe a reversal of one or two, allows the course to be changed in very little time.

The rules of the competition will probably dictate whether one or two combinations are required, and one of these must be in the jump-off.

The jump-off should have at least six jumps in it (five indoors). It is important to have a good, flowing design for this, with one or two nice turns mixed with one or two straight runs. This is the track which will decide the winner, so if you cannot find a good jump-off course in your original plan, discard it and start planning again.

Ask the show secretary for the dimensions of the ring, the position of the judges' box, and siting of the entrance and exit and the collecting ring.

Remember to have the **first jump** – maybe the first two – towards the collecting ring, to get the horse going. Try to put the **last jump** in the region of the exit, to save time on the day if there is a large entry.

If there is no timing equipment, place the start and finish lines level with the judges, as this will help them to use their stopwatches more accurately.

Pre-plan the courses at the 'drawing board',

preliminary designs.

If stopwatches have to be used, it will help the timekeepers if the start and finish lines are level with the judges' box.

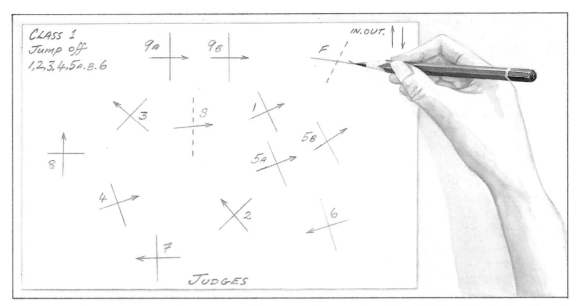

Draw your first course on a large piece of paper – A4 is ideal. Use pencil so that you can easily make alterations. Draw arrows to denote the direction of each jump, numbering them on the take-off side. If the judges' box is shown along the base, the plan will be the correct way up for the judges to read.

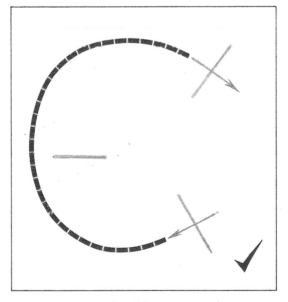

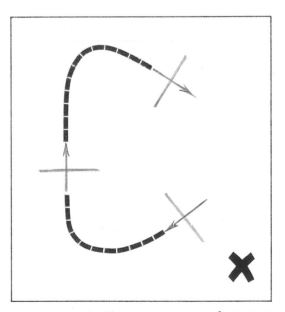

The horse must be able to approach every jump comfortably at a nice, even pace. If a rider is forced to slow down to negotiate a corner, the fence must be badly sited at too acute an angle. This is poor course designing. All courses should be straightforward and flowing.

Master plan

It will simplify things on the day if you have a master plan showing all the different courses on one sheet of paper. To do this, take your first course plan and, using a different colour pen, add to it the numbering of the jumps for the second plan, writing the fence numbers on the take-off side. Don't add arrows, unless bringing in a fresh obstacle, as this will only cause confusion during building. Continue adding later courses, colour coding as you go. Once the master plan is complete encase it in a clear plastic folder to keep it clean and protect it from the weather.

Once you have planned your tracks, decide which jumps will be uprights and which will be oxers, mixing them well to keep the horse interested and alert. The first fence should always be an inviting ascending oxer, which is the easiest jump, to get the horse going well.

Give a copy of the master plan to any assistants.

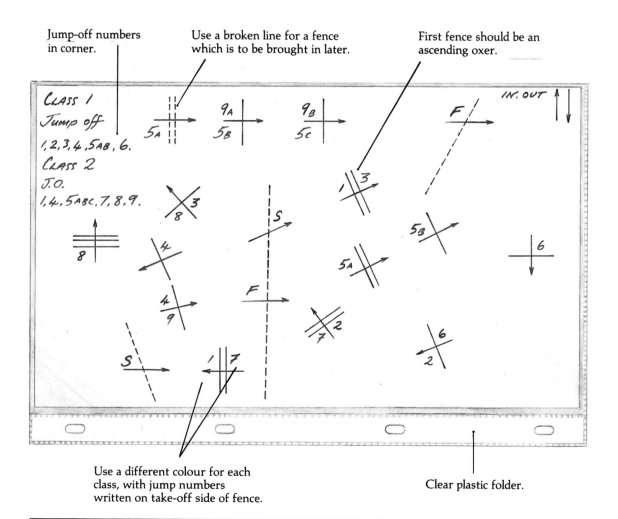

Jump-off numbers in corner.

Use a broken line for a fence which is to be brought in later.

First fence should be an ascending oxer.

Use a different colour for each class, with jump numbers written on take-off side of fence.

Clear plastic folder.

Building the course at a show

You will need a measuring tape, a measuring stick (6½ft/2m if possible) and wet-weather clothing. It is usual to build the course the day before the show, and the organisers should arrange for the fence material to be delivered to the site in readiness. If the jump wings have been transported without their feet on, ask for a gang of helpers to put them on before you arrive, to save time.

The jumps may be a hired set, or they may belong to a club or private individuals. Look at the material you have, and decide what will be going where, making notes on the master plan. Start by putting a pole down in the exact position that you want to place each jump. It is much easier to adjust the angle of a pole than to move a completed fence. Make sure that there is plenty of room at either end of the ring for the horses to turn.

If you have two jumps fairly near to one another, pace out the distance between them in multiples of four of your own (3ft/90cm) strides. This will ensure that the distance will ride on a fairly true stride, but bear in mind those factors on page 12 which can affect the stride lengths.

When you have laid out all the poles, stand back and ask yourself whether you could possibly drive a car round the track. If you think you could, then the course should not present difficulties for a horse.

Next, move the relevant material to the poles, including the cups. Leave a few spare poles (neatly) round the edge of the ring, ready for when the jumps go up in height and in case of breakages.

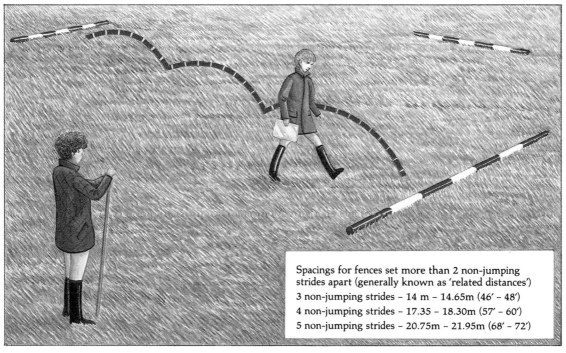

Spacings for fences set more than 2 non-jumping strides apart (generally known as 'related distances')
3 non-jumping strides – 14 m – 14.65m (46' – 48')
4 non-jumping strides – 17.35 – 18.30m (57' – 60')
5 non-jumping strides – 20.75m – 21.95m (68' – 72')

Building the course (contd)

With the materials at hand, the frame can now be built to the height and spread required. The schedule will usually state the maximum height for each class, but the final decision as to whether to build to the maximum rests with the course designer, who should take into consideration the quantity and quality of the entries.

Once the frame is built, it is then filled in. To a certain extent, clear rounds can be regulated with safety, by the positioning of the filler, as shown below. Poles placed close together, so long as they are not jammed by the cup above, are easier to jump than those spread wider apart. Square parallels are harder to jump than ascending ones, especially after a slightly shorter distance.

Fence numbers should be placed on the right.

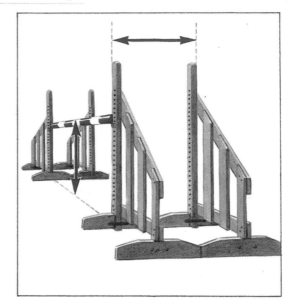

The frame and how to measure it.

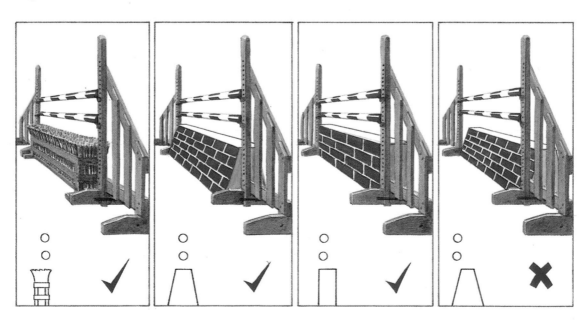

Easy   Harder   Difficult   NEVER

Plans for judges etc.

A course plan has to be supplied to the judges, and another displayed in the collecting ring, with the relevant details for each class. All the information shown below must be included. (Do not draw a continuous line as this implies a compulsory route, deviation from which would result in elimination. The only time this would ever be used is when you elect to force a particular turn.)

A measuring wheel will be needed if the class requires an allowed time. The schedule will tell you at which speed it will be judged, and usually novice classes are run at either 300m or 320m per minute. Measure the line that you think a careful rider would take; if in doubt about whether to go inside or around a particular jump, err on the side of caution. To save time on calculations, a table of times and distances is given in the rule book of the British Show Jumping Association.

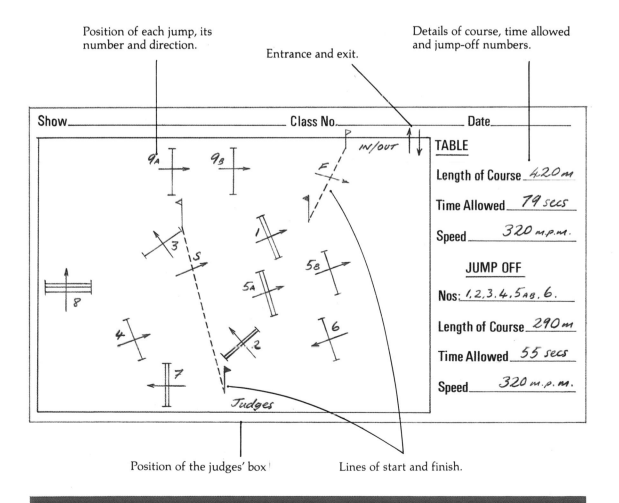

Position of each jump, its number and direction.

Entrance and exit.

Details of course, time allowed and jump-off numbers.

Position of the judges' box

Lines of start and finish.

The finished course
(as master plan, page 18)

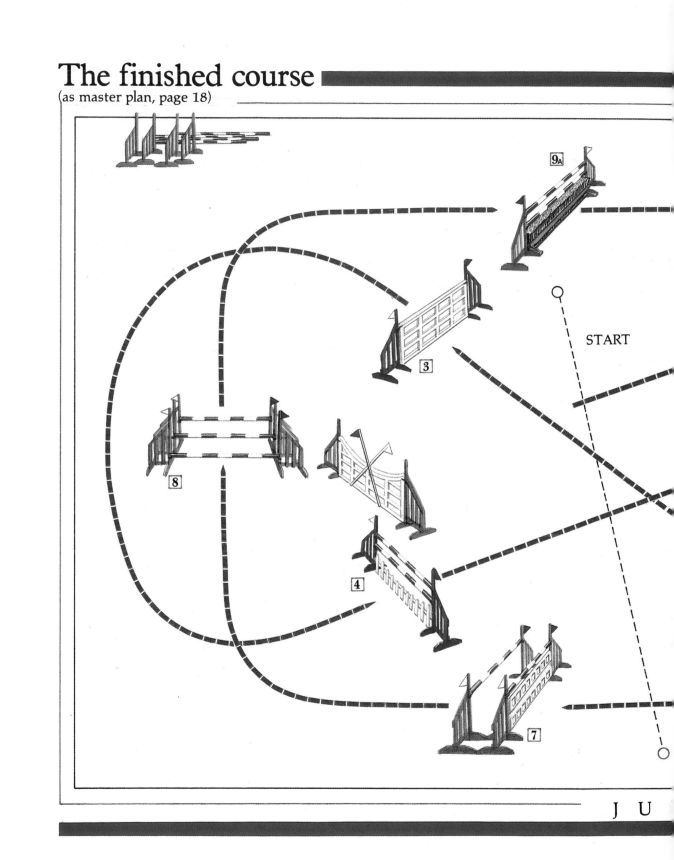

START

9A

3

8

4

7

J U

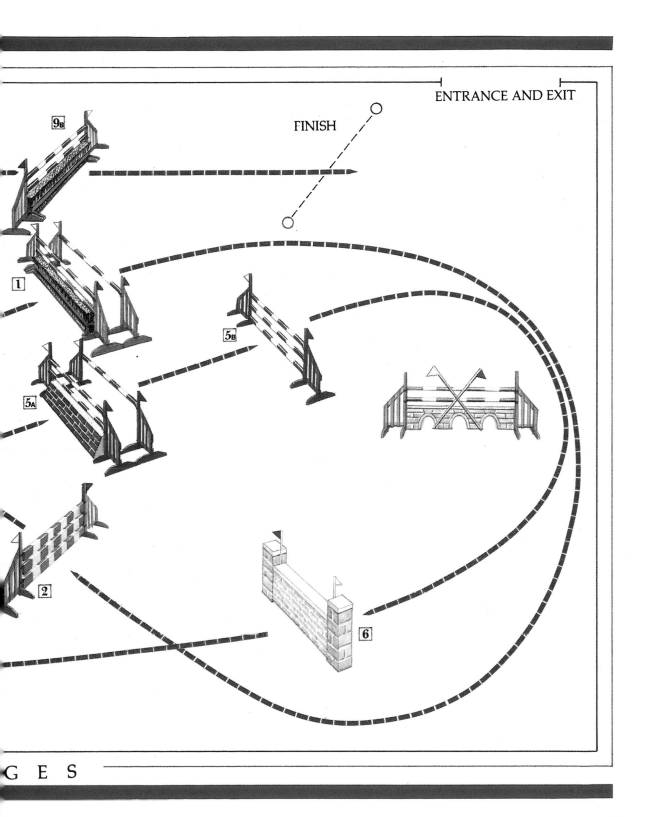

Indoor building

Courses for indoor shows require even more meticulous planning. You will need to know the dimensions of the school before you start, and the overall width of the fences. To design the course to scale and to make sure that your course will fit the arena, it is helpful to have some graph paper and some matchsticks cut down to size. Courses intended for a restricted area should always be kept straightforward with extra attention given to the creation of easy turns.

The distance that the jumps are built from the end of the school is very important too – they should never be closer than 45ft (13.50m). There will have to be more related distances between obstacles built indoors, but the table of distances on page 19 can be safely used, providing that you lean towards the shorter distances. The same applies to combinations.

Conclusion

Coursebuilding is hard work, but this can be minimised with careful pre-planning. Safety is the most important aspect, but it is also vital to assess the ability of the competitors, so that you build to make a good class with the right result. Also, there will be spectators, so the course should be made as attractive as possible, making use of whatever decorative material (e.g. foliage and flowers) is available. Above all, it is very rewarding to watch a fine-looking horse jump a stylish, free-flowing clear round over a course that you have designed and presented yourself.